Time Is Shorter

THAN IT'S EVER BEEN BEFORE

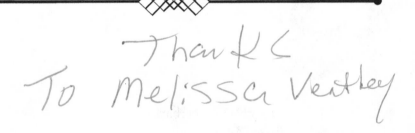

To Melissa Ventley

Thanks

WILLIE JILES

ISBN 978-1-0980-4322-3 (paperback)
ISBN 978-1-0980-4323-0 (digital)

Christian Faith Publishing, Inc.
832 Park Avenue
Meadville, PA 16335
www.christianfaithpublishing.com

Printed in the United States of America

ACKNOWLEDGMENTS

To my mother, Rushie Jiles, and my daddy, Bill Jiles, for raising me in a church and teaching me to believe that God is, and he is, a rewarder of them that diligently seek him (Hebrews 11:6).

And to my wife, Janet Jiles, for her assistance and encouragement to write this book.

May God bless the readers.

Contagious
Common Sense

I thought everybody was crazy by the way their time was spent. They did not love one another and did not care where anyone went. They depended on a computer to trace the money they spent.

And I was one of those people when I found my common sense. I remember it was arrested by order of the president. I heard that he died on the Internet. The truth was his defense.

Convicted of loving his neighbor, his conviction made no sense.

God said that all men are of one blood, and that's just what he meant. He had a purpose for all things, and he loaned us common sense.

Well, I was at the graveyard when they buried common sense. His loved ones all got flowers and all the good will that was sent. I touched him in his casket, and I went to my residence. I started feeling really strange, so off to the doctor I went.

He said, "Son, you have been infected with contagious common sense."

It's a very rare condition that common sense possessed. It was passed on to you from the body that the common sense had left. So now that it's in your thinking, it will be there to lead you on.

It is contagious, but it is not deadly. And you can pass it on. You can give it to your neighbor and give it to your friends. I hope that you can infect everyone and make common sense common. Again.

Poem: Cities with Songs

I was down in Alabama with "Georgia on My Mind." I left my "Sweet Home Alabama" locked in jail but didn't do no crime. My noisy cellmate sang, "My Darling Clementine." They caught him with cocaine on the *Macon County Line*. He got a lawyer down in Memphis called the Candy Man. If anyone can free him, the Candy Man can.

The warden's lady was from down in the boondocks. The warden said he saw her one day in New Orleans sitting on the dock of the bay. It was hard for him to get her. She left her heart in San Francisco. The arresting officer was not on my side. He said he thought he saw me "The Night Chicago Died."

I tried to remember last night when I was "Rocky Mountain High." I was on the "Last Train to Clarksville" and caught a "Midnight Train to Georgia." I remember the "Brooklyn Road" looking for "Philadelphia Freedom" and went to "Detroit Rock City," but it was West I had to go. So I started looking for direction to El Paso headed South through LaGrange and saw an Okie from Muskogee and stopped in Tupelo.

Tupelo, honey, gave me money, and I was still on the go.

Wind got high and the weather got stormy. I promised a Californian girl an "Amarillo by Morning." I hit Luckenbach, Texas, on the way to Abilene. I met a "Little Old Lady from Pasadena" and told her I was lost and "Do You Know the Way to San Jose?"

The "Wichita Lineman" came and gave me the news, not "Viva Las Vegas" but the "Folsom Prison Blues." By the time I get to Phoenix, I'll have a new attitude. I called up my lawyer. I had to make a deal. He said he would get me free in a bar in Bakersfield.

Western TV

I was on my way *West* on *The Laramie Trail*. I went through the *Big Valley* past the *Men from Shiloh*. I traveled on through the wind and rain. I spent two nights on the *Wagon Train*. There was a girl from last night named *Calamity Jane*. I saw Gene Autry and Roy Rogers on this side of Dodge City. From there, I got on the Arizona trial and spent some time with the cannons on the *High Chaparral*.

Billy the Kid came through. He was on the lam. They said he was running from a real bad lawman. He just stopped by, and then he was gone 'cause the man chasing him was Wyatt Earp from Tombstone. There was a gunfighter there that said his name was Shane. He was looking for some trouble from *The Rifleman*. I've heard a lot of stories of *How the West Was Won*. There are *Mavericks* out there who live by cards and guns.

A cowboy died, and in Doc Holliday's opinion, the man died from being slow, and he was not *The Virginian* they had bounty hunters then. A lot of money was spent, and *Have Gun—Will Travel* was called Paladin.

He tracked Frank and Jesse James and didn't make a cent. He caught many men wanted—dead or alive. They were on the run. They on *Boot Hill* now from a *Restless Gun*.

Some died for a *Bonanza* on the *Ponderosa* and didn't have a dime in their pocket when their lives were over. A lot of men have died, and it isn't no joke. They on *Boot Hill* now, cause of death: *Gunsmoke*.

RAGGY ASS CLOTHES

There are sophisticated people with raggy ass clothes. I remember when I was young (my stories must be told), I was really poor back then, didn't have many clothes. My mama put the patches on most of our old clothes. Back then, you didn't wear pants or shirts with a whole lot of holes. I had pants, shirts, and coats with patches over all my holes.

School children always laughed at me about the holes in my clothes. They laughed even louder about the shoes that I wore. They had cardboard in the bottom and cotton in the toes. They were the ones my big brother could not wear anymore.

I was told the way to tell the rich from people who are poor. It is by the number of patches and holes in their clothes. I was really young back then, a lot of things I did not know.

Now people are paying big money for raggy ass clothes. Now the world is in reverse from what I was told. Only poor people go around with holes in their clothes. It's hard for me to believe when I go into the store and see the high, high prices on raggy ass clothes.

They are faded, they are ripped, and for big dollars they are sold. You can buy a brand-new suit that has rips, tares, and holes.

They look like the ones I wore to school when they laughed and called me poor. Now I can't afford the high prices of them raggy ass clothes.

I Lived Another Day

I think of things that happen to me along life's way, of what some people thought of me and the words they had to say. Some said, I could not succeed. They said there was no way. Some tried to defeat me. On my journey day by day, they had the idea in their heads because I'd ran away. To their surprise, I came again to win another day.

I believe what people say about quitting and running away. A wise man will come again to fight another day.

I was not in the battle slain. I'm still around today 'cause he who's in the battle slain will never rise to fight again.

Enemies tried to keep me down, many stood in my way. Somehow, I got around them all. I lived another day.

I've loved and been loved all my life. I know I cannot stay. I think I got this far in life by what Jesus had to say. He said, "I am the truth. I am the light. I am also the way."

I think that is why he lets me live. I've lived another day.

Long as I live, I thank the Lord. It's not all happy and gay. I thank the Lord that I woke up to spread some love today.

God has given me his grace. I've lived another day.

Because I'm a Jiles That's Why
(A family name poem)

I can do all things through God who strengthens me. All I have to do is try. Because I'm a Jiles, that's why. Jiles—the name is legend, and legends never die. I'm a living legend. I am going to tell you why. Because I'm a Jiles. That's why.

You can knock me down. You may even make me cry. You can never stop me. I'm reaching for the sky because I'm a Jiles, that's why. I can rule the world and build castles in the sky.

I can have all the things that money can buy. And because I am a legend, I'm going to tell you why because I'm a Jiles, that's why. I have a Lord and Savior; he says I'll never die. I tell you that I believe him. Let me tell you why. Because I'm a Jiles, that's why. I know you have never seen a legend, but you are looking at one now.

You see me with your eyes. And your eyes can't deny. I'm Jiles and I'm a legend. I already told you why.

All the way from slavery to my mansion in the sky. Jiles—the name is legend, and a legend will never die because I'm a Jiles, that's why.

Payday

You are working for payday on the job you're working on. You get up early in the morning, work till the day is done.

You work really hard to make payday come. There is pay for every work and every good thing you've done. You'll pay your bills with money when payday comes.

It means lots of dollars but little for some 'cause they don't volunteer when the overtime comes.

You got a good job, and you work hard every day. You get time and a half for overtime pay.

Just living this life is a job every day. When you leave this world, you'll get the big payday.

Did you work for the Lord? Did you walk in his way? Did you help out your neighbor when trouble came his way? Did you trust in the Lord? Did you walk in his way? Did you stay on the job, never late any day? Did you get yourself ready for the big payday? Because for all the deeds that you've done and all the words that you've said, there's a God in heaven. He will give you your pay.

When your life on earth has ended and you go on your way, you'll see God face-to-face; it's the big payday.

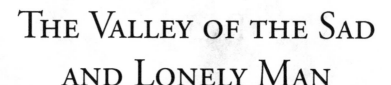

The Valley of the Sad and Lonely Man

The valley of the sad and lonely man, that valley is a low place between high places, lower than some can understand.

A cold lonely place, full of troubles and mind quicksand is known as the valley of the sad and lonely man. There is a place in the valley; it's lonely and still. You realize you are lonely from the way your spirit feels.

You know that you are alone, and you don't understand. You have a notion that this event, it was not planned. You have arrived in the valley of the sad and lonely man.

The place is dark and still and cold as the night between a valley and a hill.

There is evil in the valley. It will try to take your hand and lead you deeper in the valley of the sad and lonely man. Way down deep in the valley, you will never find a friend. It's the law in the valley of the sad and lonely man.

You can leave the valley and go to other lands. If you can find the exit, then you can make a plan to get out of the valley of the sad and lonely man. I know there is an exit. I can find it. Yes, I can, then I will leave forever the valley of the sad and lonely man. I have been through the valley, don't have to go again.

I survived the empty valley of the sad and lonely man.

THE NEW PRAYER WARRIOR

In an old, old house, there was a woman alone. In the quietness of the nighttime, twilight was gone. A sound broke the silence, a scream. And a little boy was born.

When the lad learned to pray, he was crawling on his knees. That was when he heard his mother pray. "Lord, have mercy on him please."

The world was full of wickedness, sorrow, sin, and scorn. And it was too busy to notice that a prayer warrior was born.

The child grew closer and closer to God. His way was always weary, his tribulation hard.

He called on the father and learned about the son. Time became his enemy. His precious mother was gone on.

His years were lived in sorrow. His prayers became more bold. He rose from prayer one morning and realized he was old, fell back to his knees, and prayed for more lost souls. And the child born after twilight knew his youth was gone.

Although his days were filled with sorrow, the prayer warrior prayed on. At last, time overtook him. Like at birth, he died alone, and the angels came and took the old prayer warrior home.

The prayer warrior's life was ended. I know he is gone, but his last prayer was answered; a new prayer warrior's born.

WHAT PRECIOUS
MEANS TO ME?

My precious one I'll love forever. A precious love beyond all measure. A love especially for me. Let me tell you what's the key (that's what precious means to me).

A precious love I'll always treasure. A love I mean to keep forever. A love especially for me (that's what's precious means to me). *Precious* is a word, you see, that tells all love the heart can see. A love meant only just for me (that's what precious means to me).

Like only God can make a tree, my heart made you precious to me. A precious love I'll always keep (that's what precious means to me). No other love can ever be than precious love you gave to me. The strongest love a heart can see (that's what precious means to me). And by my love I want to be, let me tell you what's the key (that's what precious means to me). A greater love can never be than what my precious gave to me. I hope by now that you can see just what precious means to me. No greater love can ever be than what my precious gave to me (that's what precious means to me). No greater love can ever be than that my precious gave to me. That's what precious means to me.

OPPORTUNITY TOMORROW

When opportunity comes tomorrow, not a visitor comes to stay.

It comes sometime in the morning, and it's gone by the end of the day.

I had opportunity this morning, and none at the end of the day.

You hear the sirens blearing, do you ever pause to say sounds like a life's in trouble, someone's having a really bad day?

They might have to live with their troubles, may have to beg and borrow and pray.

I hope they believe tomorrow is still another day.

Opportunity is like tomorrow; it will not come to stay.

If ever you get to tomorrow, you will have resurrection day. And like opportunity, tomorrow is still a day away.

If your miracle is coming tomorrow, you know it's on the way. I'll be safe on tomorrow, that's when I'll get my pay.

So I will see you tomorrow, if you can't find me here today. I'm gone into tomorrow. I finally found the way. I took the opportunity to get saved on yesterday.

You Can't Kill
a Dead Man

I have cancer. Cancer does not have me.

I possess cancer. Cancer does not possess me.

I have to live with the cancer as long as I can.

Cancer cannot kill me. I'm dead in Christ.

Understand? Cancer cannot kill me. You cannot kill a dead man.

It may be put on a paper that cancer is why I died.

But I am dead in Christ already, and like Jesus, I will rise.

I don't know what killed Lazarus. The Word said that he died. But when Jesus call him to come forward, he came out of the tomb alive.

Martha came to Jesus and said he shouldn't have died. He said, "Whosoever liveth and believes in me, they shall never, never die."

So when you come to bury me, I hope you understand.

My birth, my life, and living are still in my Savior's hand.

Jesus was killed and died for me and rose to life again.

I'm already dead in Christ, and you can't kill a dead man.

God's Training Camp

I woke up this morning in God's training camp. I was sad and lonely. My spirit felt all cramped. Lord, I got made over in God's training camp. You ought to come on over to God's training camp. You can get made over in God's training camp. Angels are all around you in God's training camp. Holy spirit came and found me in God's training camp. I got a broken and contrite spirit. In God's training camp, you ought to come on over to God's training camp. There is joy and salvation in God's training camp. You ought to come on over to God's training camp.

There Is a Light
beyond the Clouds

If you got a trouble in your life, there is a light beyond the cloud. Steven spoke to sinners; they got angry. And they got loud when they took the stones to kill him. He saw a light beyond the clouds. Jesus came to live among men, and for our sins, he died. Rose again and ascended, he's the light beyond the clouds.

In this life, you will have tribulations, and you'll also have trials. Lift your heart and eyes to Jesus. He's the light beyond the clouds. If I died before the trumpet, I know I'll hear the shout because I believe in the name of Jesus. He's my light beyond the clouds. One day, you'll hear the trumpet blows. The angel will give a shout, that's the mighty voice of Jesus. He's the light beyond the clouds.

The Hat on Daddy's Head
(Dedicated to Dad, Mr. Bill Ely Jiles)

He did not wear his hat in the house. He did not put it on the bed. But whenever Dad left the house, he had a hat on his head. He took it off when he came back home. And he wouldn't wear it to bed.

He wouldn't tell me a lot of things. I'd talk too much, he said. There were a lot of things that I didn't know under the hat on Daddy's head. I really talked a lot back then, just like my daddy said. There was a lot of knowledge under that hat on Daddy's head.

He told me, "Son, a man is a man. There are people in this world with riches in their hand that think the color of their skin is what makes them a man. They live lives of luxury, racisms in their heads. They don't know equality."

It is what my daddy said. A man is a man eternally. From the living to the dead, there was also taught humility from the hat on Daddy's head.

When times were bad within our lives, my daddy always said, "I know the Lord will make a way," and we were always fed. Now I am old and living free with food and plenty of bread. I'll always have prosperity because of what my daddy said. I'll never have all the wisdom from the hat on my daddy's head.

Gold Is Just a Rock

April 13, 2019

You may make billions of dollars on Facebook and Amazon stock, but there's so much gold in heaven that they call it just a rock. There are a lot of millionaires making money on market stock. They have insider trade knowledge; they hide it in their socks. For those who have a love of money, they make the market rock. They have billions of dollars and treat people like livestock, but they won't be happy in heaven where gold is just a rock. They rule and run some nations with all the money they got. They rule and hide their evil. God's Word, they refuse to know. Money is the root of all evil, and money, they think, is better than gold. They heap money together. They want to have more and more. They won't be rich in heaven. They will be paid for all of their stock. To all the souls on the streets of heaven, gold is just a rock.

Break Time

I went to my job with a Monday headache. I had to work really hard before I got to prebreak. I took an aspirin to help my headache 'cause in fifteen minutes, it will be first break. Aspirin kicked in at the end of my break. The fifteen minutes left is called post-break.

I worked hard. I didn't do a bunch 'cause in a few minutes, it will be time for prelunch. Prelunch fifteen is over, and I ate a whole bunch. Lunchtime is over. I enjoyed my lunch. I got fifteen minutes left. And that's post-lunch. I got one more break by the end of the day. Prebreak then break. Post-break is on the way. That's the last fifteen-minute break before the end of my day. Prebreak is fifteen minutes, and break is fifteen minutes too. The third fifteen minutes is post-break. And it's true. When you're working on a job, take the breaks you are due.

A Flea Fell Out
of the Tree

I was walking through the woods hunting strawberries. I put turpentine on to keep the red bugs off me. I was wearing sunscreen to keep the sun from burning me. I wore my sunglasses. They were dark, but I could see. I didn't start itching till I waked under a tree. I looked all around to see what was itching me. I looked at my arm, and it was hard for me to see a little jumping black dot turned out to be a flea. It was the cause of my itch; a flea fell out of the tree.

COMPANY MAN

There are a lot of employers trying to find the right man. He must follow company instructions, swear an oath and a pledge. He must follow all directions, and he must understand all of the duties of a company man.

He must follow orders, not steal or rob 'cause he knows it's the end of his company-man job. When he sees the boss, he will put a smile in his face 'cause he don't want to lose his company-man place. He takes all the credit for things he didn't do. And everybody knows he's a company man too. He works mostly with his mouth and not at all with his hands. He doesn't have to work; he's a company man.

He's the star employee and he don't miss a day and he loves everything that the boss man says. When the overtime comes, he's the first to raise his hand. He always tells the boss, "I'm a company man." He watches all the things that the other workers do, and he'll sneak around and tell the boss on you. So when you get your new job, you need to put it in your plan to be on the lookout for the company man.

ALL TO JESUS GLORY BE

This is a poem about Jesus on how he was born and died for me. Now I lift my voice to heaven and say to Jesus, "Glory be."

He was born among the best and crucified on Calvary. And to the Lord, all glory be. He shed his blood for a wretch like me, for my sins, transgressions, and iniquities. That's why to Jesus glory be. He got off that cross on Calvary. Now he prepares a place for me in his home in glory, where I will be, and so to Jesus all glory be. So to God all glory be.

God's Miracle to Me

The miracle of life was bestowed on me by God. I've learned from his word what he wishes for me. To live every day to its fullness when he gives them to me. He gave me a companion to live with me and to love me in good times and bad; she shows her love for me. We were each one without union, and now it's we. She stands with me in my decisions, no matter how wrong or right they all may be. She treats me like a mother and sometimes like a child, lifts me up from discouragement with just a smile. She's the best friend I'll ever have in my life. She is my partner. She's my pal. We try not to have strife. She is the best thing that ever happened to me in all of my life. She is the woman that I chose to be my wife. I will always love Janet. She brings happiness to my life because she is my wife.

Bragging on Jesus

May 2, 2019

The worker is bragging on the weekend. The mail person is bragging on the mail. The fireman is bragging on the water. The police is bragging on the jail. But I'm just bragging on Jesus 'cause he saved my soul from hell. The banker is bragging on the money. The bondsman is bragging on the bail. The salesman is bragging on payday and money from the things he sells. But I'm just bragging on Jesus 'cause he saved my soul from hell. The funeral home is waiting on dead folk. The doctor, he's bragging on the well. But I keep bragging on Jesus 'cause he saved my soul from hell. The winners all brag on winning. And the seller is bragging on the sale. And I keep bragging on Jesus 'cause, he saved my soul from hell. The lost all brag on Jesus when he saves their souls from hell. So keep on bragging on Jesus when he saves your soul from hell. So I keep bragging on Jesus 'cause he saved my soul from hell.

A Song about Me

I came to Jesus just as I was weary, wounded, and sad. I found in him a resting place, and he has made me glad. That's a song about me. They wrote a song about me. Just as I am without one plea, but that thy blood was shed for me. That's a song about me. They wrote a song about me. Amazing grace, how sweet the sound that saves a wrench like me. I once was lost, but now I'm found. I was blind, but now I see. That's a song about me. They wrote a song about me.

There is a fountain filled with blood that flows from Emanuel's veins. A sinner plunged beneath the flood lose all their guilty stains. That's a song about me; they wrote a song about me.

THINGS YOU ARE DUE

Everybody wants to get the things they are due. You try to live right by the things that you do. And when you use your words, they all are true. But when you wake up one morning, and there isn't any dew, and the world clouds up and rains on you. When you are out of money, and the rent is due. And you can't find the good friends that you once knew. The loan at the bank and the car note is due. You can't go to the doctor because the insurance is overdue. There is thunder in your life, rain and lightning too. And you don't think that these things are due for you now. You are working at night and part-time too. You are learning that life is in the things that you do. Now the car note is paid and the insurance too 'cause you kept on pushing. When life rained on you, you didn't give up until the storm was through. You don't know what is next in life for you. But you know that it will be the things that you are due.

SAME WORD,
DIFFERENT MEANING

Some say hay. That's the stuff for horses. Some say hey. It means hello, hi. Some say rat, and that's a rodent. I say it's right there for you. Some say far, and that's a distance. I say far means fire. Some say patient, and that's a person. Some say patent; it means the time you are waiting. Some say by; it means goodbye. It also means what your money can buy. Say it another way; I'm glad you came by. Some say sun; that's the bright shining light. Men say son; that's a father's delight. Some say see for the letter *c*. That's not the same things that your eyes can see. Some say get up and stand, but you have to sit down on time witness stand. I hope you get my meaning. I know you can. It's not the some meaning as milk in a can. Of all the word that we all know, the number one word is no means no.

Jesus Wept

On the day that Lazarus died, Martha, Mary, and the Jews all cried. While in the grave, Lazarus slept. The Bible says, "Jesus wept." Martha came to him and cried. If you were here, he wouldn't have died.

Jesus said unto her then, "Thy brother shall rise, rise again. I'm resurrection, and I am life. Whosoever lives and believes in me, he shall never, never die."

Mary came and kneeled and cried, "If you were here, he wouldn't have died."

On the day that Lazarus died, Martha, Mary, and the Jews all cried while in the grave, Lazarus slept. The Bible says, "Jesus wept." He called Lazarus forth to rise, but it was after he had cried. Jesus wept. The savior wept. My Lord, he wept. Jesus wept (John 11:15).

Time Is Shorter than It's Ever Been Before

Jesus is standing at your heart, and he is knocking on the door. Let him in. Let him in. It will soon be time to go. The angel of God will give a shout, and we will hear a trumpet blow. That is the time the church is leaving. The Savior's grace will be no more. Time is shorter than it's ever been before. Tell your father. Let him know. Tell your mother. Let her know. Tell your brother. Let him know. Tell your sister. Let her know. Tell your friends. Let them know. It will soon be time to go. Time is shorter than it's ever been before.

THE BEND IN THE ROAD

I was running down life's highway, sinning all the time, when I went around the curve, I came upon this sign. It said a few more miles down to hell's country line.

But there's a bend in the road. My way was twisting and turning. My life became a heavy load; I could not see where I was going. There was a bend in the road.

My life became a heavy burden, and there's a friend I could not find.

When I went around the bend, Jesus held up a sign. He said, "Turn right here. I will lighten up your load, put you on the road to heaven from this bend in the road."

Well, I took the road to heaven, lots of valleys and hills to climb.

But I got to keep on running. I just saw another sign; it says a few more miles up to heaven county line and ain't no bend in the road. There ain't no bend in the road. Jesus found me at the bend in the road.

Like People Used to Do

People used to do the math. They could add two and two. Now we have a calculator, makes answer right and true. Now they don't have to do the math like people used to do. Some have a robot in their home; they tell it what to do, and it can do most of the things that people used to do. Technology, in our new world, always has something new. It counts the money when you shop and tells your change that's due. They get it right most of the time like people used to do. Now you can talk on a telephone. You see them, and they see you. It's not the same as face-to-face like people used to do. We make a deal and shake our hands like people used to do. Now you need a piece of paper. You need a lawyer too. You will see things in this life. They may be strange to you. You may not see the shaking of hands and a kind "How do you do?" But those are the things we do no more like people used to do.

TEACH YOUR CHILDREN
HOW TO PRAY

When Jesus came along this way, disciples ask him how to pray. This is a prayer a child might say when they bow down to God and pray: "Father, lay me down to sleep. I pray thee Lord my soul to keep. If I should die before I wake, I pray thee Lord my soul to take. And this I pray for Jesus's sake."

Before you go along your way, teach your children how to pray. Teach them first God's face to seek. Teach them all God's Word to keep. So they have peace when they are sleep. Teach your children words to speak before you go along your way. Teach your children how to pray.

God is Ever Ready

April 24, 2019

Not like a battery, he never needs recharging, but we are ever ready for the things life brings to be. Life brings springs mornings. You see birds up in the trees. Life brings you all the songs they sing to you and me too. Life brings the noonday, sun so hot you want to flee. Life brings every evening, the sunset for you to see. Life brings trials and troubles so dark you cannot see. So deep down in your soul, you want to cease to be. You need to have trust in the Lord. He needs no battery. He'll keep you in his love. He is ever ready. When troubles come your way from ways you cannot see, there is a Lord that's full of love. He needs no battery. When I fall down, he lifts me up. He is ever ready through all my trails along this life. I know he pleads for me saying, "If you trust me and my Word, you will never cease to be."

So I take Jesus at his word. I call it a guarantee. I believe all of his promises and the blood he shed for me. I will live on. My soul is saved. God's power will not leave me. It will take me all the way to heaven.

My God is ever ready.

BEHIND THE
HIDE BEHIND

You cannot see the hide behind; that is why he hides behind. Back in the woods, you cannot find. No one who's seen the hide behind. There are stories of people dying. The way they died were not kind. And so they blamed the hide behind. They're hunting for him all the time. All day, they're looking back and behind, but you can't see the hide behind. I told it to a friend of mine.

He said, "I can find him anytime," and now he hunts the hide behind. I told him that with me that's fine, but you can't find the hide behind. He's a real good friend of mine. He is so good, and he is kind. And in the world, you will not find a friend that you can hide behind. You want to see me doing fine, just look behind the hide behind. I hide behind the hide behind.

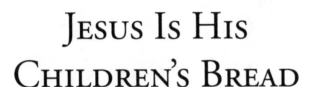

Jesus Is His Children's Bread

I look up to heaven, and I bow down my head. I thank you, Lord, for children's bread. Jesus is his children's bread. He casted out a demon from a child upon her bed with just a crumb of children's bread. Jesus is his children's bread. He died on the cross. He came back from the dead to give his children bread. He is his children's bread. He healed the sick, and he raised up the dead. Jesus gave them children's bread; Jesus gave his children bread. He is his children's bread.

GOD'S WORD
DON'T CHANGE

In the beginning was the Word and the Word was with God and the Word was God. The same was in the beginning with God. He don't change. God's Word don't change. If my people, which are called by my name, would humble themselves and pray and turn from their wicked ways and seek my face, then will I hear from heaven and forgive their sin and heal their land. He don't change. God's Word doesn't change. If you forgive, he will forgive. Obey God's Word, and you will live. He don't change. God's Word doesn't change. God's Word, he don't change.

The Leaving of the Dreams

When the morning comes, the dream, it has to leave. When you go to sleep at night, your mind withdraws into itself to a land of beautiful dreams. You are impressed within yourself in a happy world you can believe. You find the life you want to live; that's what your mind believes. You sleep with a smile upon your face for the happiness you receive in a world of love and joy that you have never seen. When you are suddenly jarred awake, daylight has come indeed. And always, when the morning comes, the dream, it has to leave. The joyous vision in your mind, your life was filled with glee, they are all gone. Morning has come, and the dream, it has to leave. You had the sun upon your face, the wind and a gentle breeze. But once again, morning has come, and the dream, it has to leave. One day, you hope to sleep and dream with all the beautiful sense, and on that day, morning will come, but the dream will never leave.

WORKING ON THE DREAM

There was a man named Martin who told the world about a dream, a dream of freedom and justice, a dream of things unseen. He wanted a world without hate. He said to let freedom ring. He was a man of spiritual power; he was Martin Luther King. Before his life was ended on a mountain, top he'd seen that those that would survive him would keep working on the dream. Through the years, some things have changed. He would be proud to represent the USA had a black president. Civil rights for everyone was a dream of Mr. King. Now we have different colors, different lifestyles, and themes females running for president. They are working on the dream. They are standing up for righteousness. They are working on the dream. They are working on equality. They shout to let freedom ring. The world must remember the dream of Doctor King: keep working on the dream.

WHEN A MAN GOES OUT

When a man goes out, is it the way that he goes? Was he drowned in the water or get hit in the nose? When he left, was it from an overdose? Or did he go in the way that a bad man goes? Did he have an ID for the tag on his toe? There are a lot of people dead, they are called John Doe. Every man got to leave. Did he died in bed, trying to make his life to go? Or was he a bad man trying to get some more doe? Well, he's good and dead now, and the pall bearer knows, but he doesn't know yet why the man had to go.

There's an answer to the question that I want to know. When a man goes out, is it the way that he goes? And the women too also have to go. They are in the morgue too with a tag on their toe. Their gravestone says their name was Jane Doe. When the undertaker man puts the tag on your toe, it won't make no difference about the way that you go. You'll be good and dead, then you won't have to worry anymore.

THE SPIRIT OF CHRISTMAS EVE

Like a warm wind that blows right before the spring the faint smell of flowers of the evening breeze, so is the anticipation that comes on Christmas Eve.

Little children are restless is their glee. They all wait for Santa Claus to come on Christmas Eve.

The spirit brings hope to those in need and makes other people, with all their love, do many wonderful deeds.

The spirit was born from a star so bright that led wise men to Jesus on a dark starry night. The spirit, it was pleased, but on Christmas Eve, it went away at the start of a brand-new day. Then Christ came into the world. He's in our hearts to stay. The spirit of Christmas Eve had gone along its way.

He made a way for all mankind's eternal life that day.

The son of God came to the world. We call it Christmas Day.

The Refrigerator Light

The light is always on when I open up the door.

It illuminates the shelves so I can see where my food goes.

I thought it was still on when I went down to the store. But the shelves were all dark when I opened up the door 'cause the refrigerator light was not on anymore.

The light bulb was blown. I had sense enough to know, so I put a new one in that I got down at the store.

So when I want to thaw some meat to make myself some grub, I put my frozen food under the refrigerator light bulb.

I replaced the bulb, and the light is on to stay, thawing out my frozen food by the night and by the day.

So to thaw your food in the fridge, there is a very simple way: put it in front of the bulb and the ice will go away because the refrigerator light is on both night and day. So open up the door; you'll see just, why I say the refrigerator light is on both night and day.

What Does the Dishwasher Do?

Tell me what in the world does the dishwasher do?

I know the fridge light is on. I open up the door, and it keeps right on shining when I close the door.

The washing machine washes clothes, and the dryer dries them too.

The stove cooks food; it is done when it is due. But what in the world does the dishwasher do?

People wash dishes and dry them too before they put them in the basket of their dishwashing tool.

You get into the shower, get clean with soap and water, dry off with a towel, put on deodorant too.

Is that the same thing that the dishwasher do?

The remote turns on the TV and changes channels too, even fixes the color with a button or two.

Tell me, is that the same thing that the dishwasher do? I know about the dryer and the TV too.

I know the refrigerator light is always on for you.

You wash the dishes with your hands, the pots and pans, too, so will you tell me what is left for the dishwasher to do? So what does the dishwasher do?

THE ROAD TO CANDY LAND

Mary Jane went walking down Candy Lane and met a honeybun there. They both caught a train. The train crossed the border to the State of Sweets.

They left the train down on Zero Street and saw Mr. Keebler chasing down a little Debbie running from a moon pie. He lost her when she turned the corner of Butternut Lane. Mr. Good Bar picked her up on Butterfinger Road.

The girl was tired. She had ran so hard, asked to be dropped off on Snickers Boulevard. She caught a bus from there going to Almond Joy Town. The bus had to stop in the State of Mounds. She went to the airport riding a Tootsie Roll where the Reeses Plane took her to the City of Peeps. She met a Kit Kat bar with peppermint in his hand, told her to take the subway down to Candy Land. Three musketeers will be waiting at the gate.

She found Candy Land, and to tell you the truth, she found her sugar daddy there named Baby Ruth, gave her a black cow sucker and a bunch of kisses too.

They got married by a preacher on Hershey Boulevard. The honeymoon in Dove Chocolate Land left no maybe. In the spring, there will be a sweet little sugar baby.

In the Lower Side of Heaven

There is a love money can't buy in the lower side of heaven. An angel, there will call your name when God says, "Come up hither." You will receive your full reward from our father who art in heaven. Everything is love and joy at the throne of God in heaven. You better hope that you get in to the lower side of heaven. The only way to go is up to the heaven of all heavens.

LIFE GETS BETTER
WHENEVER I PRAY

As I go along life's highway trials and troubles, they come my way.

But life gets better whenever I pray.

I thank you, Lord, whenever I pray. I thank you, Jesus, whenever I pray.

I know you died. I know you rose. You paid a debt, Lord. You never owed.

Since you rose up, Lord, from the grave, I owe a debt I can never pay.

You make life better whenever I pray. My load gets lighter whenever I pray. My path grows brighten whenever I pray. My life gets better whenever I pray.

Soap Operas and TV Shows

I was walking through the twilight zone at the edge of night, searching for tomorrow.

I stumbled into another world; they took me to a general hospital.

I was seen by the doctors at the ER.

The good doctor said, "It was the strangest things we have ever seen. In all the days of our lives, it was totally outer limits."

THE UNBORN

No matter why a child is unborn, God has his love for everyone.

The unborn goes to heaven. Some are born learning right from wrong. And some of their lives are suddenly gone. Some rise in hell; some rise in heaven. The unborn go to heaven. They don't learn hate or scorn. The unborn go to heaven.

The unborn ones, they have no sin. They don't have to worry about getting in. The unborn's home is in heaven.

THE NIGHT BEFORE FIFTY

September 15, 2018

It was the night before fifty, up in my house.

The old age thing bothered me, but I couldn't say it out.

I asked the pharmacist about my pressure pills. They said, "Don't you remember that one was already filled?"

I was good in all my twenties, thirties, and even in forty-five. Still.

But something about big fifty gives me funny little chills.

I got all my medication. It might give me a thrill. It has to work for me by midnight in the halls of my mind. I'll have a wonderful life at fifty that I didn't have at forty-nine. When I wake up in the morning, big fifty will be mine.

The Slow Gentle Rain

If you ever survive a hurricane, you remember the thunder, lightning, rain, storm surge, and deadly tornadoes. Not to mention those who are caught in the floods, the real loud bangs and the unknown thuds.

The same thing happened, the clouds bring rain every time before and after the hurricane.

Well, there's a lot of fear of the stormy rains. There is a sweet sleep and part of the proof.

When slow gentle rain falls on roofs of tin, the people get drowsy in the houses they live in.

The gentle pitter-patter upon the ground is like a lullaby with the sleepiest sound.

The rain rides on the wind and in the high treetops, rocking ever so gentle like a cradle rocks.

When I hear the rain on my housetop, I rock in my chair like a cradle rocks, and now in my dreams, there is no fear or pain. I sleep in the land of the slow gentle rain.

Fast Food

Papa John's was playing Domino's with little Caesar's over at Pizza Hut. With hungry Howie's, they all went to lunch at Popeye's with the Burger King, and they are all going to White Castle's churches with Ruby Tuesday's. To make things Krystal's clear, Ryan's, Denny's, and Captain D's were not invited due to Arby's refusal to eat fish at Hardy's on Friday's. McDonald's could not come. He was arrested at Sonics for Dunking Donuts with Krispy Kreme.

It happened after Dr. Pepper diagnosed Coca-Cola got crabs at Red Lobster. Doc also said that there were signs of infection of pancake from Waffle House.

There will be further information after lab results from Taco Bell. We also need the coroner's report from KFC. In other news, there is an investigation into whether or not Golden Corral's A-salted big mac and Beef 'O' Brady at Checkers as reported by ole Charlie's in the fast-food recipe book from Smokey's Pit Bar BQ. This report is sponsored by what a whopper at www.whatawhoper.com address chillis chillis chillis Rosie O'Grady's Boulevard in fast food Florida Phone # 222 fast food 4 u.

THE LOVE LETTER

This is a love letter, not a birthday card, a greeting, or get well soon to make you feel better.

This is a love letter. An expression of my love for you, not a rose, not a violet, and not a poinsettia. This, my virtuous woman, is a love letter.

When my eyes first saw you, my heart said, "You must get her. With all of her charm and beauty, you have to become much, much better."

My mind said, *She is so beautiful.* I thought, *How can I get her?*

And that is when it came to me. Try writing your love in a letter.

This is a love letter, not a charm, not a gift or a hat filled with a feather.

This is a love letter. But I cannot speak this face-to-face. I hope you read this letter.

This is a love letter. No matter how low I am and no matter what the weather, the sight of you within my eyes always makes life much better. That's why, dear loved one, I'm writing you this letter.

This is a love letter I've wondered, thought, and pondered too. What in the world am I to do to let you know that I love you, but write the words I know are true in this love letter just for you?

This is a love letter just for you.

DRAMP

May 4, 2019

I went to the shower to get myself clean, grabbed a towel to dry off, if you know what I mean, not a wet or damp towel. It was in-between.

So I used the darn thing to get my body clean. Now the towel wasn't wet or damp. It was in-between.

It was a darn damp towel. It got my body really clean. It's what the aliens use on the planet of dramp and treasured, like gold, is a towel that is dramp.

It was told by Od the God of Dramp. He declared the temperature in his world to always be dramp—not hot, not cold, not wet or damp. Somewhere in-between, it will always be dramp.

You don't cook in the summer and in winter. Don't freeze when it's dramp. All around you, there is always a breeze. You'll feel the drampness in the air that you breathe.

Everything around you is always clean. It's not wet or damp. It is in-between. On the planet of Drampness, you always stay clean. You get wet, get dry, and you can get damp, but there's only one place in the world that you can get dramp. It's in the atmosphere on this planet of Dramp.

THE PRINCE OF PEACE

Jesus, the prince of peace of mind, I sing his praises all the time.

Author of love and joy divine.

I love the prince of peace of mind. He put his love in this heart of mine.

Jesus, the prince of peace and mind, he is the key to this peace of mine.

I sing his praises all the time.

Come to the prince of peace of mind and find the cause of this peace of mine.

Joy's in my heart all of the time, author of love and joy divine.

I sing his praises all the time.

I love the prince of peace of mind.

Come to the prince of peace of mind.

Too Blessed to
Be Cursed

Working on my job and going to church, looks like my trouble increased and my burdens got worse. Somebody even said I was living under a curse.

I know I pray to God, pay tithes, and go to church.

I know I read my Bible. I study it, verse by verse.

I found that I'm a child of God. I'm too blessed to be cursed.

So I might still have trouble, my situation may get worse. But as long as God's love lives in me, I'm too blessed to be cursed.

Look What I Found in the Word of the Lord

Look what I found in the Word of the Lord. I found joy. I found joy in the Word of the Lord.

Let me down, let me down in the Word of the Lord. O, look what I found in the Word of the Lord. I found love. I found love in the Word of the Lord.

Let me down, let me down in the Word of the Lord. O, look what I found in the Word of the Lord. I found peace. I found peace in the Word of the Lord.

O, look what I found in the Word of the Lord. Let me down, let me down in the Word of the Lord. I found faith, rest, and grace in the Word of the Lord. Lord, o, look what I found in your Word. Lord, let me down, let me down in your Word, Lord.

Make Me a Man after God's Own Heart

In the garden from the start, God made a man after God's own heart. His flesh was weak, like it is now. Back then, that's the reason sin sneaked in.

Jesus loved me from the start and died for my sins. He did his part to make a man after God's own heart. Make me a man after God's own heart.

Now I pray to do my part to be a man after God's own heart.

Make me a man after God's own heart.

Only See the Colors of God's Grace

When you judge a person from the color of a face, you choose then not to use the color of God's grace.

We come into the world to God's predestined place. His commandments told us to love one another without regard to the face.

He made all men of one blood regardless of their race. When you judge by reason of color, you lack God's saving grace.

So when you judge by reason of color or the skin on a person's face, remember the Word of the Lord, the saved are saved by grace.

Bad Hair Day

I jumped out of the bed and started on my way, got my hair in place with my perm hair spray.

The sun was shining, looks like a real pretty day. Then it got cold, and it rained that day.

Humidity got high, and my spray went away.

Wind blowed so hard that my wig flew away.

Somebody said it was a bad hair day. I got really tired, and my hair turned gray.

I almost lost my mind by the end of the day. My gray turned loose and went away to stay, and I don't worry no more about a bad hair day.

SHORT OF YOUR GLORY

Father, I have sinned, and I come short of your glory.

You cried for me, but I'm short of your glory. You died for me, but I'm short of your glory.

And you rose for me in all of your glory, all of your glory, all of your glory, Lord. You'll come for me in all of your glory, all of your glory, all of your glory, Lord.

Prayer is All Right

When trouble comes in to cloud my mind, prayer is all right all the time.

When life comes to a mountain you think you can't climb, prayer is all right at that time.

When the world comes to you with the hardest times, prayer is all right at that time.

Your problems have you in a bind. You need the Lord; it's praying time.

Prayer is all right all of the time. Prayer is all right all the time.

Jesus Is

You need God's Word to do God's will. I'll give it to you, Jesus is when you are hungry and can't be filled, eat the bread of life, and Jesus is you thirst for water so you can live drink the living water that Jesus is.

You need a judge for your case to hear.

You need a doctor for your heart to heal.

I'm here to tell you, Jesus is. You need a friend to dry your tears. There is a friend who's always near.

I'm here to tell you, Jesus is. Rock of salvation, Jesus is. Bread of life, Jesus is maker and creator. Jesus is the living water. Jesus is Alpha and Omega. Jesus is; he always was. He always is the son of God. Jesus is.

TRIAL BEFORE THE THRONE

There is a day of judgment by the judge upon the throne.

The court he will call to order. You are accused there all alone.

To get the payment for your works, you did your whole life long.

The payments will be itemized now that your life on earth is gone.

Payment will be rendered to you about your rights and wrongs. Did you have love for God's mercy before you came before the throne? Did you always judge rightly? Did you always walk humbly even when times were hard? If so, you'll have your case dismissed when you're at the throne of God.

He said for you to do justly and for you to love mercy and walk humbly before your God.

It's written in the book of Micah for you to understand.

You can never be convicted when you do the whole duty of a man (Micah 6:8; Deuteronomy 10:12).

HEAVEN'S TRANSPORTATION

April 13, 2019

The souls you meet in heaven will all be equal souls. You only love your way to heaven. You get there along love's roads.

There is a road map to heaven, a transportation for your soul. When you believe in the Lord Jesus and the stories that are told, how he died and went to heaven and the transportation that he rode.

On the Friday before Easter, he departed. In love's transportation he rode, set down with the father in heaven, who told him where to go. He came back on love's transportation on Easter morning. When he was alive, he arose. Love is God's transportation.

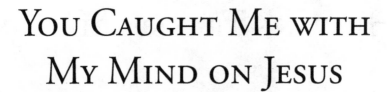

You Caught Me with My Mind on Jesus

Woke up this morning with my mind on Jesus. Stopped to pray, had my mind on Jesus. Went on my way, kept my mind on Jesus. You caught me with my mind on Jesus. Worked all the day with my mind on Jesus. You caught me with my mind on Jesus. Now I am walking with my mind on Jesus. And now I'm talking with my mind on Jesus. At the end of my day, I have my mind on Jesus. And now I pray to keep my mind on Jesus. You caught me with my mind on Jesus.

ALL IS WELL

My testimony, I must tell. While on my journey along life's trail, I sometimes stumbled, sometimes fell. My testimony is all is well. Jesus found me. I had fell to him, all of my troubles I tell. My testimony is all is well.

He saved me from a burning hell, forgave my sins, and I must tell, my testimony's all is well. Then says my soul all is well.

LIKE JESUS

I want to walk like Jesus walked. I want to talk like Jesus talked. I want to pray like Jesus prayed, and I want to do what Jesus said. I gotta cry like Jesus cried. I gotta die like Jesus died. I'm gonna rise like Jesus did. And I'm gonna go where Jesus is.

So I gotta walk like Jesus walked, and I gotta talk like Jesus talked. I gotta pray like Jesus prayed, and I gotta do what Jesus said. And after I cry like Jesus did and after I die like Jesus did, then I'm gonna rise like Jesus did. Then I'll go where Jesus is.

The Old Prayer Warrior

There is an old prayer warrior that I know that all his prayer to heaven go. And when he prays and the results won't show, the old prayer warrior prays some more, for the sick and burdened and those with woe. He lays his prayer at heaven's door. Until they get answered, he prays some more. He prays in the rain. He prays in the snow. He prays over the roads and wherever he goes. He even prays on the radio.

The old prayer warrior's a good friend to know. When you are down and out and your trouble won't go, just find a way to let him know. And the old prayer warrior will pray some more.

The power in the name of Jesus, he knows. So he knows where his prayers go. So when you have troubles and they won't go, find the old prayer warrior, and he will pray some more.

LETTER TO THE OLD PRAYER WARRIOR

I knew he had not heard from me.

He might have thought my troubles were gone.

So I sent a message to him that my troubles lingered on.

I really hated to bother him; he had troubles of his own.

But I had to write and encourage him and ask him to pray on.

I know I pray for you myself and make supplications on my own.

But I believe the prayer warrior's prayer always reach the throne. Yes, I still pray with you for all of your troubles to be gone.

But if all our prayer were answered, there would be no reason to pray on.

We will always pray for each other; all our troubles are never gone. So keep on praying for me. I believe the Holy Spirit takes your prayers to God's throne.

So pray on, prayer warrior, pray on.

I Know What the Lord Loves

The Lord loves a cheerful giver. The Lord loves a holy liver. The Lord loves for you to love one another, honor thy father and honor your mother. I love the Lord's love. I love the Lord loves, and I love the Lord's love. The Lord's love is a holy deliver, a soul saver, and eternal life giver. I love the Lord is love. I love the Lord loves. I love the Lord's love. I know what the Lord loves. The Lord loves love.

Father, Forgive Them

When Jesus was dying on the cross, he said, "Father, forgive them for they know not what they do."

He said, "Father, forgive them."

He was talking about me too. I said, "Father, forgive them for the nails they put in your hand with the hammer of my sin."

I said, "Father, forgive them for the thorns they put in your head."

I said, "Father, forgive them. It was me who should have been dead."

I said, "Father, forgive them for the stripes they put on your back."

I said, "Father, forgive them. I believe you are coming back."

Father, forgive them.

The Ole Dirt Road

I was born back in the woods along an ole dirt road. My siblings used to tease me. They said I was not their brother; I was found beside the road.

I asked my mama and daddy. They said that it was not so. There were other people that live on the ole dirt road—Miss Lily on top of the hill and Big John lived on a knoll.

There were some funny times walking down the road. A man named JT had a whip. When we met, I'd cross the road. Miss Bessie always went fishing down at the fishing hole. There was a wooden bridge on buckhorn creek and cow pens on the side of the road.

The blossoms from magnolia trees often fell in the road. Sometimes I'd see a wobbly trail where a snake had crossed the road. I walked the road sometimes at night, and bobcats crossed the road. Now and then, a car came by on the dry and dusty road. There was a dust so thick it was like walking in a cloud.

A lot of cars slid in the ditch on that wet and slippery road. We played baseball on a field full of stumps and holes. A man came weekly in a bus. We called the rolling store two cookies for a penny, and for two cents, we got four.

I walked many miles in barefoot and got sand cuts in my toes. I seldom saw the black top at the end of the ole dirt road. The days of my young life are spent; they are gone now. I'm old. My heart is filled with fond memories from our days on the ole dirt road.

THE OLDER I GET, THE BETTER I WAS

The older I get, the better I was keeping up with the boys, as well as the girls. I had it like that kissed all the girls. I was drinking the water, drank a little wine, kicking up dust, having a wonderful time, but my transporter broke and I cannot find the backup button that make it rewind.

I remember the time hanging out with my cousin. I was ruling them all; that's how much better I was. Well, I'm older now, so I hang out with old folks.

They are old people here of every kind. They all looking back trying to find their rewind. My body don't remember, but my mind sure does. You see, the older I get, the better I was.

I would go back again, have a good old time, but my transporter's broke. I can't go back in time. I need the backup button to make it rewind.

The boys get old, as well as the girls, and the older I get, the better I was. Oh dear God, would you be so kind as to make me like I was? Send me back in time. I'll be better than I was when I find the rewind.

I will see myself like my memory does. You see, the older I get, the better I was.

Babies Grow Up to Be People Too

Children grow up watching what people do. Babies grow up to be people too. When children grow up, they do what parents do. When they're on the way up trying to be people too. They learn how to act from what grown people do. They see how you act and hear what you say too. And they try to do things the same way you do.

They see you doing wrong and hear you lie too. Now what in the world do you expect them to do?

They see the bad things that grown people do.

If you have a little baby, I want you to know that you should train up a child in the way they should go. And when they get older, they'll know where to go.

Babies grow up. I don't care what you do. Teach them right; they are watching you because babies grow up to be people too. Babies grow up to be people just like you.

Babies grow up to be people too. When babies grow up, they are watching you. Babies grow up to be people like you. Babies grow up to be people too.

THE LAST HOUSE ON BUCKHORN CREEK

There's a man they cannot find on the buckhorn creek. As a baby, he was found by the banks of the creek, down in the woods where there aren't no streets.

Now the man was born and raised on the backside of the woods, where he got his food the best way that he could. He ate possums, coons, and squirrels when he caught them, and he could. When his mama cooked it up, it was darn sure good.

He worked the ground for his greens and potatoes to eat, and you could always get some fish out of buckhorn creek.

The cow gave milk and butter that was sweet, and he could catch wild hogs down buckhorn creek.

At night in the woods, the moon shines like day, and it lights up the trail so the man can find his way.

His daddy told a story about how he got a scare. Lost his gun one night, running from a big ole bear. He went back the next day 'cause he left his gun there. He found a big black tree and said it look just like a bear.

So if you go into the woods on buckhorn creek, there are some strange things there that you don't want to meet. So don't pass the last house on buckhorn creek. If you pass that house, the only thing that you might meet is the man they cannot find on buckhorn creek. So when you walk through the woods and something touches your cheek and you get so scared that you can't speak and your knees start to tremble and you can't move your feet, you have found the lost man on buckhorn creek. It's the end of the line. There is no one else for you to meet 'cause you passed by the last house on buckhorn creek.

THE FUNERAL OF COMMON SENSE

I was at the funeral. I mourned because he is gone.

I depended on him all my life to influence the right from wrong.

Today, the world is in a dangerous place since Common Sense is gone.

His wife was at the head of the funeral procession.

She is in failing health; her name is Discretion.

His mom, Truth, was there. His dad, Trust, too. They had lost all of their hope, and they were dying too.

His girl child mourned and looked really weak. Her life is leaving also. She's Responsibility.

When Common Sense was buried, it was the end of his long season. His legacy will die. It's up to his son, Reason.

Reason has got married to a girl. Her name is Hope. She is having twin babies, one boy and one girl.

The boy's name will be Patience. The girl's name is Love.

They will show their granddad's message to a distressed and confused world. Perhaps their children's children will bring common sense back to the world.

Looking for the Lord

April 27, 2019

When you are looking for the Lord, you're always looking up.

If you think you are going to heaven, then you have to be looking up.

You know hell is down, so you need to be looking up.

You are humble on your knees. You want your prayers to go up.

So don't send your prayers down, you want them to go up.

When you're sending out your praises, your praises go up.

When our Lord and Savior died, he had to first go up.

When he died, he was in hell. Took the keys to hell and death, and then he rose back up.

No matter how low you go in life, I hope you keep your trust in our Lord and Savior who went down and came back up.

He is our hope of glory, and glory it is up.

God says there is a heaven of heavens, and heaven is up.

He says, "The dead in Christ, are sure to go up first?" And we who remain, shall surely be caught up.

So don't forget the hope of glory, and glory's always up.

When you're looking for the Lord, the Lord is always up.

ABOUT THE AUTHOR

Willie Jiles always wanted to be a songwriter. The poems he presented that mention God and Jesus are from his reading of God's Word for which God gets all the glory. The rest is from the trails in his life, which he's hoping would bring a smile to the reader's face.

Every new day you live in this lifetime makes your lifetime shorter than it's ever been before.

He is sixty-five years old, and writing will always be a hobby of his. He hopes that the readers enjoy the poems in this book and tell other people about it. He loves writing and will continue to every day that the good Lord lets him see the sunshine. Always love God and put him first in your life, and he will provide you with all the blessings.